"The earth a...

Prayers, Blessings, Principles of Faith, and Divine Service for Noahides

adapted from

The Divine Code

by

Rabbi Moshe Weiner

Including daily prayers authored by

Rabbi J. Immanuel Schochet

"for My house shall be called a house of prayer for all the nations." (Isaiah 56:7)

Editors:

Dr. Michael Schulman, *Director*
Chaim M. M. Reisner, *Founder*
Ask Noah International
Cover design by Laurel Tessmer.

ISBN 978-1-7323735-1-8 (*7th Edition*)

© 20'18-20'23 by Ask Noah International
All rights reserved.

No part of this publication may be translated or reproduced without prior permission in writing.

Information requests may be addressed to:
Email: SevenLaws@asknoah.org
Internet: https://asknoah.org

Other books from Ask Noah International:

The Divine Code, 4th Edition

Seven Gates of Righteous Knowledge

To Perfect the World (pub. S.I.E.)

Go(o)d for You: The Divine Code of 7 Noahide Commandments

*Prayers for Noahides:
Community Services and Personal Worship*

CONTENTS

Introduction ... 4

I. Principles of Faith and Divine Service

Awareness of God, and the Noahide Path ... 6
Serving God with One's Mind and Heart ... 9
The Power of Personal Repentance ... 15

II. Recommended Prayers and Blessings

Daytime Prayers ... 16
Evening Prayers ... 37
Blessings Before Eating or Drinking ... 43
Other Blessings of Thanks to God ... 46
Rules of Blessings for Foods or Beverages ... 47
Grace after a Meal ... 50
7 Verses for Noahide Children to Learn ... 53

III. Prayers for Specific Needs and Requests

Prayer for Livelihood ... 55
Prayer for Travelers ... 57
Prayer for a Sick Person ... 58
Prayer for a Newborn Gentile Baby ... 59
Prayer for a Departed Soul ... 59

Please guard the sanctity of this prayer booklet.

Introduction

The universal obligation to pray is to ask for one's physical needs, but the true main purpose is to connect with the Creator. A constant connection with God is also an essential human need – that God should be with a person in all his ways (and all of his ways should be fitting for this connection). The prayer itself is a connection, made through conversation, requests, and praises to God, Who hears the prayer of all and also provides this spiritual need.

A main part of prayer is concentration on the greatness of God and the Truth of His Existence, to set these ideas in one's heart, in all areas of life.

Gentiles have no set liturgy of prayers which they are obligated to follow. Rather, each individual can pray to the One God in his own words, in a language that he understands. It is proper to include recitation of excerpts from the Book of Psalms by King David, of blessed memory, since the Psalms are all prayers to God that were composed with holy inspiration and encompass all the essential needs and righteous spiritual emotions that people have.

The importance of charity boxes:

Placing coins for charity into a can or small box in one's home is encouraged for Gentiles as well as Jews. By giving any amount before praying, a person can benefit from this extra merit. The Divine service of charity dates back to Abraham, as God said about him (Genesis 18:19): "For I love him [Abraham] because he commands his children and household after him that they shall keep the way of God to do charity and justice…" Giving properly directed charity is an act of *goodness and kindness*, and Gentiles have obligations to give charity and be concerned about helping those who are physically in need. This also applies to helping those who are spiritually in need, by supporting outreach to more people locally or around the world about the Torah's Noahide Code.

Part I

Principles of Faith and Divine Service[1]

Awareness of God, and the Noahide Path

The basic foundation and the first principle of faith is to know that there is a Primary Being who brought all existence into being. All of the entities in the spiritual and physical realms come into existence only from the truth of His Being. This Being is the God of the universe and the Master of the entire earth. He controls the spheres and the entire universe with infinite and unbounded power that continues without interruption. This God is one, and only can be one, and not two or more. He is one with a complete unification that surpasses any of the types of unity that are part of the created

---

[1] This is a brief listing of major principles of Torah-true faith. For further explanation of these concepts, and in more depth, see *The Divine Code*, Part I (Fundamentals of the Faith).

realms. He is completely unified, and there exists no unity similar to His within the created realms.

God's ability and power have no limitation or boundary. His power is not the power of a body, and He does not have a body or any form.

Just as His Existence is of an entirely different nature than that of the created beings, so too, His Truth is incomparable to their truth. For all the created beings require Him, and He, blessed be He, does not require them.

The obligation of this knowledge is not only to understand this precept once and to agree and set it in one's heart. It is a continuous obligation for a person to think about and contemplate the existence of the Master of the universe and His greatness in order to set this knowledge strongly in his heart and mind. One should constantly reflect upon this, as the righteous King David wrote, "I place God before me always; because He is at my right hand I shall not falter."[2] This recognition of the existence of God includes acceptance of His Kingship and His constant authority.

With awareness of this knowledge and that God created this world for people to live together righteously in His Presence, one is obligated to accept upon himself God's commanding of the Seven Noahide Commandments (listed briefly on the back of this booklet) and their details as transmitted in the Torah. Any Gentile who accepts these commandments and is careful to observe their details is truly pious and merits an eternal portion in the future World to Come. This applies only if he accepts them and does them because the Holy One, blessed be He, commanded them in the Torah, and made it known through Moses our teacher that Noah's descendants were previously commanded to fulfill them.[3]

---

[2] Psalms 16:8.
[3] Maimonides (Rambam), *Mishneh Torah, Laws of Kings* 8:11.

Serving God with One's Mind and Heart

It is incumbent on every person to try to achieve understanding of the Creator according to his capability, and he should meditate always on the greatness of the Creator, and on His supervision over the whole creation, in order to awaken his heart to love and fear Him.

What is this love and fear? When a person understands that God is the Creator of everything and keeps everything in existence at every moment, and that God created all people so they should honor and serve Him, and then he meditates on the infinite greatness of God according to his ability and understanding, he will come to love God.

When one also contemplates the lowliness of any creation in comparison to the Creator of everything, he will realize God's infinite greatness, and awe and fear of God will fall upon him. A person will also be humbled by knowing that he is a small, lowly creation with severely limited understanding, who is standing in the Presence of God Almighty.

Also included is the effort a person should make to follow correct paths and deeds that will be pleasing to God, even if there are no specific commandments that apply. God expects that if a person is blessed with the opportunity to learn of these ways, he will strive to follow them. The Prophets of the Hebrew Bible revealed that these are ways of kindness, justice, mercy, righteousness, graciousness, and humility. One should also focus his mind and heart, so that his actions will be in accordance with God's will.

Included in the obligation to believe in and recognize the Creator of the universe is the trust that a person must place in God. With this trust, a person must have faith that God is surely concerned about him, and about all of His other creations, and that everything God does is for the ultimate good of the person, since God is the ultimate good. One aspect of this trust is that each of God's commandments will in truth be for the good of the person who is so commanded, and it is for the good of the entire world.

The main part of this service of the heart and mind is prayer. Therefore one should always pray before God, to make requests to Him for all of his needs, and he should thank and praise Him always according to his ability. Another goal of this prayer and contemplation is to bring the person to know that there is nothing worthy of complete trust except the One God, Who is King of the universe.

When a person prays, he should clearly express his words to God with his lips in speech if possible, and not only in his thoughts, so that he will earn the merit of doing a good deed in the service of God.

A person can pray at any time of day, and in any fitting words that he chooses. But he should be careful not to use prayers that idol worshipers composed for their liturgies, and he should not pray to God if he is in a house of idol worship.

One's prayers should be said honorably, in order to honor God. Therefore, it is meritorious to pray in honorable clothing. One should not pray in filthy clothing, or unclothed, or in the presence of others who are unclothed. One should also not pray where there is a bad smell, or in a lavatory or bathing room, or within about 6 ft (1.8 m) of excrement. If one is standing in a place where other people are unclothed and he must make a request to God, and he has no option for another opportunity to pray, he should turn his body (or at least his head) in order not to see them, and then pray. If this is also impossible, and in the above situations, if there is a great need to pray but one is not able to move to a place that is acceptable for prayer, it is better to pray in one's heart, and not say God's Name in such a place.

In the same way that a person should praise and bless God for all the good he receives, and recognize that these things are from Him, likewise it is an obligation to recognize that hurtful and painful things one experiences are also directed by God. One should know and acknowledge that the ways of God are beyond understanding by mankind. Everything that God does with a person is in truth an opportunity for the good of the person, as it says (Psalms 145:17): "The Lord is righteous in *all* His ways."

Every person has natural traits, and there are other traits that one acquires by regularly habituating himself to act in these ways. A person must always evaluate his traits and strive to bring them toward the correct path.

One must especially strive not to become angered or to be an angry person. If one is naturally an angry person, he should train himself to act with humility and patience toward others by habit, until he permanently acquires these good traits. Likewise with other character traits, one should evaluate himself truthfully to determine if he acts as a righteous and charitable person would, and he should correct himself to act in a way that finds favor in the eyes of God and in the eyes of other people.

Therefore, using containers at home, at work and in one's car for depositing coins for proper charity is greatly encouraged. Gentiles may do this on a daily basis, even many times a day and on any day. The Sages taught, "Great is charity because it brings the Redemption closer."[4]

Kindness and charity can be done on many levels. A person should not mistakenly view the act of giving as only a kindness to others, since the act of giving is more beneficial to the giver than the recipient. Anyone who has pity on the poor is pitied by God. Therefore, a person should meditate that he is constantly requesting from God to provide him with the necessary livelihood, health and all other good things in life, and just as one depends on God to listen to his prayers, so must one answer the requests (and prayers) of the poor. One who has mercy on others is given mercy from Above, but one who closes his eyes and ears from the cries of the poor should not wonder why it seems that God is not listening to him.

---

[4] Tractate *Bava Batra*, p. 10a. This applies if the charity money is not given to, or collected for, any causes that are in violation of any precepts within the Torah's Noahide Code.

The Power of Personal Repentance

Just as a person needs to examine his actions to see if they are sinful, and repent from those which are, he likewise needs to search his personality for the bad traits he has, and to repent from those also and correct his ways – such as traits of anger, hate, jealousy, sarcasm, pursuing money and honor, or pursuing physical desires and the like. These last traits are in some ways more evil than sins that merely involve action, for it is very hard to remove oneself from them. Therefore the prophet said, "Let the wicked abandon *his way*, and the man of iniquity his thoughts; let him return to God, and He will have compassion upon him; and [let him return] to our God, for He will abundantly pardon."[5]

A person should always look at himself as equally balanced between merit and sin, and the world as equally balanced between merit and sin. If a person performs one sin, he may tip his balance and that of the entire world to the side of guilt and bring destruction upon himself. If he performs one good deed, he may tip his balance and that of the entire world to the side of merit, and bring deliverance and salvation to himself and others.

---

[5] Isaiah 55:7.

PART II

RECOMMENDED PRAYERS AND BLESSINGS

Daytime Prayers

Upon awakening, a person should consider in Whose Presence he lies; he should be mindful of the Supreme King of kings, the Holy One, blessed be He, as it is said (Isaiah 6:3), "The whole world is filled with His glory."

After preparing oneself for prayer, recite:[6]

I offer thanks to You, living and eternal King, for You have mercifully restored my soul within me; Your faithfulness is great.

Lord of the universe, Who reigned before anything was created – at the time when His will brought all things into being, then was His Name proclaimed King. And after all things will be uplifted, the Awesome One will reign alone. He was, He is, and He shall be in glory. He is One, and there is no other

---

[6] From traditional *Siddur* prayer book liturgy.

to compare to Him, to call His equal. Without beginning, without end, power and dominion belong to Him. He is my God and my ever-living Redeemer, the strength of my lot in time of distress. He is my banner and my refuge, my portion on the day I call. Into His hand I entrust my spirit when I sleep and when I wake. And with my soul, my body too, the Lord is with me, I shall not fear.

Blessed is He Who spoke, and the universe came into being; blessed is He.
Blessed is He Who says and does.
Blessed is He Who decrees and fulfills.
Blessed is He Who creates all that exists.
Blessed is He Who has compassion on the earth.
Blessed is He Who has compassion on the created beings.
Blessed is He Who provides good reward to those who fear Him.
Blessed is He Who lives forever and exists eternally.
Blessed is He Who redeems and saves; blessed is His Name.

Psalms of praise:[7]

For the choirmaster with instrumental music, a Psalm, a song. May God be gracious to us and bless us; may He make His countenance shine upon us forever, so that Your way will be known on earth, Your salvation among all nations. The nations will extol You O God; all the nations will extol You. The nations will rejoice and sing for joy, for You will judge the peoples justly and guide the nations upon the earth forever. The peoples will extol You, O God; all the people will extol You. The earth will yield its produce, and God, our God, will bless us. God will bless us; and all, from the farthest corners of the earth, will fear Him.[8]

A Psalm for the thanks offering. Let all the earth sing in jubilation to the Lord. Serve the Lord with joy; come before Him with exultation. Know that the Lord is God; He has made us and we are His, His people and the sheep of His pasture. Enter His gates with gratitude, His courtyards with praise; give thanks to Him, bless

---

[7] In our translation of Psalms, we have referred to several editions including those published by Kehot and Artscroll.

[8] Psalm 67.

His Name. For the Lord is good, His kindness is everlasting, and His faithfulness is for all generations.[9]

A Psalm of praise by David: I will exalt You, my God the King, and bless Your Name forever. Every day I will bless You, and extol Your Name forever. The Lord is great and exceedingly exalted; there is no limit to His greatness. One generation to another will laud Your works, and tell of Your mighty acts. I will speak of the splendor of Your glorious majesty and of Your wondrous deeds. They will proclaim the might of Your awesome acts, and I will recount Your greatness. They will express the remembrance of Your abounding goodness, and sing of Your righteousness. The Lord is gracious and compassionate, slow to anger and of great kindness. The Lord is good to all, and His mercies extend over all His works. Lord, all Your works will give thanks to You, and Your pious ones will bless You. They will declare the glory of Your kingdom, and tell of Your strength, to make known to mankind His mighty acts, and the glorious majesty of His kingdom. Your kingship is a kingship over all worlds, and Your dominion

---

[9] Psalm 100.

is throughout all generations. The Lord supports all who fall, and straightens all who are bent. The eyes of all look expectantly to You, and You give them their food at the proper time. You open Your hand and satisfy the desire of every living thing. The Lord is righteous in all His ways, and benevolent in all His deeds. The Lord is close to all who call upon Him, to all who call upon Him in truth. He fulfills the desire of those who fear Him, hears their cry and delivers them. The Lord watches over all who love Him, and will destroy all the wicked. My mouth will utter the praise of the Lord, and let all flesh bless His holy Name forever.[10]

Praise the Lord! Praise the Lord, O my soul. I will praise the Lord while I live; I will chant praises to my God while I exist. Do not place your trust in nobles, nor in a human being, for he does not have the ability to bring deliverance. When his spirit departs, he returns to his earth; on that day, his plans come to naught. Fortunate is he whose help is the God of Jacob, he whose hope rests upon the Lord his God – Maker of heaven and earth, the sea, and all that is in them, Who safeguards truth forever. He renders justice

---

[10] Psalm 145.

to the oppressed; He gives food to the hungry; the Lord releases those who are bound. The Lord opens the eyes of the blind; the Lord straightens those who are bowed; the Lord loves the righteous. The Lord watches over the strangers; He gives strength to the orphan and widow; He thwarts the way of the wicked. The Lord shall reign forever, your God, O Zion, throughout all generations. Praise the Lord![11]

Praise the Lord! Praise God in His holiness; praise Him in the firmament of His strength. Praise Him for His mighty acts; praise Him according to His abundant greatness. Praise Him with the sounding of the ram's horn; praise Him with harp and lyre. Praise Him with timbrel and dance; praise Him with stringed instruments and flute. Praise Him with resounding cymbals; praise Him with clanging cymbals. Let the entire soul praise the Lord. Praise the Lord![12]

---

[11] Psalm 146.
[12] Psalm 150.

Blessed is the Lord forever, Amen and Amen.[13] Blessed is the Lord from Zion, Who dwells in Jerusalem; praise the Lord![14] Blessed is the Lord God, the God of Israel, Who alone performs wonders. Blessed is His glorious Name forever, and may the whole earth be filled with His glory, Amen and Amen.[15]

Our Father, merciful Father Who is compassionate, have mercy on us, and grant our heart understanding to comprehend and to discern, to perceive, to learn and to teach, to observe, to practice and to fulfill Your will with love. Enlighten our eyes in Your wisdom, cause our hearts to cleave to Your Seven Commandments, and unite our hearts to love and fear Your Name, and may we never be put to shame, disgrace or stumbling. Because we trust in Your holy, great and awesome Name, may we rejoice and exult in Your salvation. Lord our God, may Your mercy and Your abounding kindness never, never forsake us.

---

[13] Psalms 89:53.
[14] Ibid. 135:21.
[15] Ibid. 72:18-19.

*Verbally accepting God's Unity
and Kingship:*

Almighty God, we accept upon ourselves that which is written in Your Torah: "You shall know this day and take to your heart that God [alone] is God, in the heavens above and on the earth below – there is none other!"[16] We affirm the precepts of "You shall love God, your God, with all your heart, and all your soul, and all your might;"[17] and "Fear God, your God, and serve Him, and in His Name [alone] shall you vow;"[18] and, as it says, "Fear God and keep His commandments, for that is a person's entire duty."[19]

---

[16] Deuteronomy 4:39.
[17] Ibid. 6:5.
[18] Ibid. 6:13.
[19] Ecclesiastes 12:13.

For devout prayer, asking God for one's needs:

Blessed are You, God, the Supreme Being who bestows abundant kindness.

Please endow us graciously with wisdom, understanding and knowledge.

Please accept our repentance, and forgive us for our errors and sins.

Grant complete healing for all our wounds and ailments.

Bestow upon us all the needs for our sustenance from Your bounty.

Hasten the day of which it is said: "God will be King over the entire earth; in that day God will be One and His Name One;"[20] "For then I will turn the peoples to pure language, so that all will call upon the Name of God to serve Him with one purpose;"[21] and "They will not harm or destroy on all My holy mountain, for the earth will be filled with knowledge of God as water covering the sea bed."[22]

Hear our voice, God, our merciful Father, have compassion upon us and accept our prayers in mercy and favor *(other requests may be inserted)*. Blessed are You, God, Who hears prayer.

---

[20] Zechariah 14:9.
[21] Zephaniah 3:9.
[22] Isaiah 11:9.

*One may optionally say the following
Prayer of the Repentant:*

O God, I have erred, sinned and willfully transgressed before You, and I have done that which is evil in Your eyes, especially with the sin(s) of ... (*state the specific sins or errors*).

I am sincerely ashamed of my sins, and I repent and firmly undertake not to do so again.

Please God, in Your infinite grace and compassion, forgive my sins and transgressions and grant me atonement, as it is written: "Let the wicked abandon his way and the man of iniquity his thoughts; and let him return unto God, and He will show him compassion, and to our God, for He will pardon abundantly."[23] And it is written: "Do I desire at all that the wicked should die, says the Lord, God; it is rather that he return from his ways and live!"[24]

---

[23] Isaiah 55:7.
[24] Ezekiel 18:23.

For the choirmaster, a Psalm by David. May the Lord answer you on the day of distress; may the Name of the God of Jacob fortify you. May He send your help from the Sanctuary, and support you from Zion. May He remember all your offerings, and always accept favorably your sacrifices. May He grant you your heart's desire, and fulfill your every plan. We will rejoice in your deliverance, and raise our banners in the Name of our God; may the Lord fulfill all your wishes. Now I know that the Lord has delivered His anointed one, answering him from His holy heavens with the mighty saving power of His right hand. Some [rely] upon chariots and some upon horses, but we invoke the Name of the Lord our God. They bend and fall, but we rise and are invigorated. Lord, deliver us; may the King answer us on the day we call.[25]

The above Psalm may also be said whenever one is in need, as a prayer for God's help, or for God to send healing or delivery from troubles. One should mention the name of the person who is being prayed for, and be strong in faith and trust in God. Mention the person's name, even for oneself, as described below in the Prayer for a Sick Person.

---

[25] Psalm 20.

We offer praise before the supreme King of kings, the Holy One, blessed be He, Who stretches forth the heavens and establishes the earth, the seat of Whose glory is in the heavens above and the abode of Whose majesty is in the loftiest heights. He is our God, there is none else. Truly, He is our King; there is nothing besides Him, as it is written in His Torah:[26] Know this day and take unto your heart that the Lord is God; in the heavens above and upon the earth below there is nothing else.

Kingship is Yours, and to all eternity You will reign in glory, as it is written in Your Torah: The Lord will reign forever and ever.[27] And it is said: The Lord shall be King over the entire earth; on that day the Lord shall be One and His Name One.[28]

Indeed, the righteous will extol Your Name; the upright will dwell in Your presence.[29]

---

[26] Deuteronomy 4:39.
[27] Exodus 15:18.
[28] Zechariah 14:9.
[29] Psalms 140:14.

Psalms for the Seven Days of the Week

Levites sang these in the Holy Temple in Jerusalem. The first six were chosen for their relation to God's creative works on those days during the Seven Days of Creation.

Sunday: By David, a Psalm. The earth and all therein is the Lord's; the world and those who dwell there. For He has founded it upon the seas, and established it upon the rivers. Who may ascend the mountain of the Lord, and who may stand in His holy place? He who has clean hands and a pure heart, who has not used My Name in vain and has not sworn deceitfully. He shall receive a blessing from the Lord, and kindness from God, his Deliverer. This is the generation of those who seek Him, who seek Your Presence – Jacob, forever. Lift up your heads, O gates, and be lifted up, everlasting doors, so the glorious King may enter. Who is the glorious King? The Lord, strong and mighty; the Lord, mighty in battle. Lift up your heads, O gates; lift them up, everlasting doors, so the glorious King may enter. Who is the glorious King? The Lord of hosts, He is the glorious King forever.[30]

---

[30] Psalm 24.

Monday: A song, a Psalm of the sons of *Korakh*. The Lord is great and exceedingly praised in the city of God, the mountain of His Sanctuary. Beautiful in landscape, the joy of the entire earth – Mount Zion, by the northern slopes, the city of the great King. In her citadels, God is known as a stronghold. For behold, the kings assembled; they advanced together. They saw and were astounded; they were terror-stricken, they hastened to flee. Trembling seized them there, pangs like a woman in difficult labor. With an east wind You shattered the ships of Tarshish. As we have heard, so have we seen in the city of the Lord of hosts, in the city of our God; God shall establish it forever and ever. We hoped, O Lord, for Your kindness, within Your Temple. Like Your Name, O God, so is Your praise to the ends of the earth; Your right hand is full of righteousness. Mount Zion shall rejoice; the towns of Judah shall exult, because of Your judgments. Walk around Zion and encircle her, count her towers. Consider well her walls, behold her lofty citadels, in order that you may recount it to a later generation. For this is God, our God, forever and ever; He shall lead us eternally.[31]

---

[31] Psalm 48.

Tuesday: A Psalm by Asaph. God stands in the council of judges; among the judges He renders judgment. How long will you judge wickedly, always favoring the evildoers? Render justice to the needy and the orphan; deal righteously with the poor and the destitute. Rescue the needy and the pauper; save them from the hands of the wicked. They do not know and they do not understand; they go about in darkness; all the foundations of the earth tremble. I said, "You are angels, all of you are supernal beings." But you will die as mortals, and you will fall like any prince. Arise, O God, judge the earth, for You possess all the nations.[32]

Wednesday: The Lord is a God of retribution; O God of retribution, reveal Yourself! Exalt Yourself, O Judge of the earth; render to the arrogant their recompense. How long will the wicked, O Lord, how long will the wicked rejoice? They continuously speak insolently; all the evildoers act arrogantly. They crush Your people, Lord, and oppress Your heritage. They slay the widow and the stranger, and they murder the orphans. They say, "God does not see, nor will the God of Jacob perceive."

---

[32] Psalm 82.

Understand, you senseless of the people; you fools, when will you become wise? Will He Who implants the ear not hear? Will He Who forms the eye not see? Will He Who chastises nations not punish? – He Who imparts knowledge to mankind. The Lord knows the thoughts of a person, that they are vanity. Fortunate is the man whom You chastise, O Lord, and from Your Torah You teach him – to grant him peace from days of trouble, while a pit is dug for the wicked. For the Lord will not abandon His people, nor will He forsake His heritage. For judgment will bring return to righteousness, and all those with upright heart will pursue it. Who will rise up for me against the wicked ones? Who will stand up for me against the evildoers? If the Lord had not been my help, my soul would have soon dwelt in the silence [of the grave]. If I thought that my foot was slipping, Your kindness, Lord, supported me. When my worrisome thoughts multiply within me, Your comfort delights my soul. Can a throne of evil be associated with You? Those who make evil into law? They join together against the soul of the righteous, and condemn innocent blood. But the Lord was my fortress, my God, the strength of my refuge. He will turn their violence upon them, and destroy them through their own wickedness; the Lord our God will cut them off.[33]

Thursday: For the choirmaster, on the *gittit* instrument, by Asaph. Sing joyously to God Who is our strength; call out to the God of Jacob. Raise your voice in song, sound the drum, the pleasant harp with the lyre. Blow the ram's horn on the New Moon [of Rosh Hashanah], the day appointed for [Israel's] Holy Day. For it is a statute for Israel, the [day of] judging for the God of Jacob. He ordained it as a precept for Joseph when he went forth over the land of Egypt, when I heard a language that I did not know. [God says:] "I removed his shoulder from the burden; his hands were removed from the kettle. In distress you called, and I delivered you; you called in secret, and I answered you with thunderous wonders; I tested you at the waters of Merivah. *Selah*. Listen, My people, and I will attest to you; Israel, if you will listen to Me – no strange god shall be among you, neither shall you prostrate yourself to a foreign god. I am the Lord, your God, Who brought you up from the land of Egypt; open your mouth wide [with your requests], and I shall grant

---

[33] Psalm 94.

them." But My people did not heed My voice; Israel did not want [to listen to] Me. So I sent them away after their heart's fantasies, for following their own counsels. If only My people would hearken to Me, if Israel would go in My ways. In an instant I would subdue their enemies, and turn My hand against their tormentors. Those who hate the Lord would lie to Him, so their destiny will be forever. But He would feed him with the finest of wheat, and satisfy you with honey from a rock.[34]

Friday: The Lord reigns; He is clothed with grandeur; the Lord has clothed and girded Himself with might; He also established the world firmly that it shall not falter. Your throne is established from of old; You are eternal. The rivers have raised, O Lord, the rivers have raised their voice; the rivers have raised their raging waves. More than the sound of many waters, mightier than the waves of the sea, the Lord is mighty on high. Your testimonies are most trustworthy; Your House will be resplendent in holiness, O Lord, forever.[35]

---

[34] Psalm 81.
[35] Psalm 93.

For Saturday:

This Psalm is a prophetic description of the future Messianic Era.

A Psalm, a song for the seventh day. It is good to thank the Lord, and to sing praise to Your Name, O Most High. To proclaim Your kindness in the morning, and Your faithfulness in the nights, with a ten-stringed instrument and with a lyre, with singing accompanied by a harp. For You, Lord, have made me happy with Your deeds; I sing for joy at the works of Your hand. How great are Your works, O Lord! Your thoughts are exceedingly profound. A boor cannot know; and a fool cannot understand this: when the wicked thrive like grass, and all evildoers flourish, it is in order that they may be destroyed forever. But You, Lord, are exalted forever. Indeed, Your enemies, O Lord, indeed Your enemies will perish; all evildoers will be scattered. But You will increase my might like that of a wild ox; I will be anointed with fresh oil. My eyes have seen my watchful enemies; when evildoers rise up against me, my ears have heard. The righteous will flourish like a date palm; he will grow tall like a cedar in Lebanon. Planted in the House of the Lord, they will flourish in the courtyards of our God. They will still be fruitful in old age; they will be vigorous and fresh – to declare that the Lord is just; He is my strength, in Whom there is no injustice.[36]

One may also add the following Psalm:

Sing to the Lord a new song; sing to the Lord, everyone on earth. Sing to the Lord, bless His Name; proclaim His deliverance from day to day. Recount His glory among the nations, His wonders among all the peoples. For the Lord is great and highly praised; He is awesome above all gods. For all the gods of the nations are naught, but the Lord made the heavens. Majesty and splendor are before Him, might and beauty in His sanctuary. Render to the Lord, O families of nations, render to the Lord honor and might. Render to the Lord honor due

---

[36] Psalm 92.

His Name; bring an offering and come to His courtyards. Bow down to the Lord in resplendent holiness; tremble before Him, everyone on earth. Proclaim among the nations: "The Lord reigns!" Indeed, the world is firmly established that it shall not falter. He will judge the peoples with righteousness. The heavens will rejoice and the earth will rejoice; the sea and its fullness will roar; the fields and everything therein will exult; then all the trees of the forest will sing with joy – before the Lord, for He will have arrived, He will have arrived to judge the earth. He will judge the world with righteousness, and the nations with His truth.[37]

---

[37] Psalm 96.

EVENING PRAYERS

Psalms that request God's protection:

A Song of Ascents. Bless the Lord all servants of the Lord who stand in the house of the Lord at night. Raise your hands in holiness and bless the Lord. May the Lord, Maker of heaven and earth, bless you from Zion.[38] By day the Lord ordains His kindness, and at night His song is with me, a prayer to the God of my life.[39] The deliverance of the righteous is from the Lord; He is their strength in time of distress. The Lord helps them and delivers them; He delivers them from the wicked and saves them, because they have put their trust in Him.[40]

Whoever dwells in the shelter of the Most High, who abides in the shadow of the Almighty: I say of the Lord who is my refuge and my stronghold, my God in whom I trust, that He will save you from the ensnaring trap, from the destructive pestilence. He will cover you with His wing, and you will find refuge under His wings; His truth is a shield and an

---

[38] Psalm 134.
[39] Psalms 42:9.
[40] Psalms 37:39-40.

armor. You will not fear the terror of the night, nor the arrow that flies by day, nor the pestilence that prowls in the darkness, nor the destruction that ravages at noon. A thousand may fall at your side, and ten thousand at your right, but it shall not reach you. You need only look with your eyes, and you will see the retribution of the wicked. Because you [have said,] "The Lord is my shelter," and you have made the Most High your haven, no evil will befall you, no plague will come near your tent. For He will instruct His angels in your behalf, to guard you in all your ways. They will carry you in their hands, lest you injure your foot upon a rock. You will tread upon the lion and the viper; you will trample upon the young lion and the serpent. Because he desires Me, I will deliver him; I will fortify him, for he knows My Name. When he calls on Me, I will answer him; I am with him in distress. I will deliver him and honor him. I will satisfy him with long life, and show him My deliverance.[41]

A song of Ascents. I lift my eyes to the mountains; from where will my help come? My help will come from the Lord, Maker of heaven

---

[41] Psalm 91.

and earth. He will not let your foot falter; your Guardian does not slumber. Indeed, the Guardian of Israel neither slumbers nor sleeps. The Lord is your Guardian; the Lord is your protective shade at your right hand. The sun will not harm you by day, nor the moon by night. The Lord will guard you from all evil; He will guard your soul. The Lord will guard your going and your coming, from now and for all time.[42]

Lord of the universe, Who reigned before anything was created – at the time when His will brought all things into being, then was His Name proclaimed King. And after all things shall be uplifted, the Awesome One will reign alone. He was, He is, and He shall be in glory. He is One, and there is no other to compare to Him, to call His equal. Without beginning, without end – power and dominion belong to Him. He is my God and my ever-living Redeemer, the strength of my lot in time of distress. He is my banner and my refuge, my portion on the day I call. Into His hand I entrust my spirit when I sleep and when I wake. And with my soul, my body too, the Lord is with me, I shall not fear.[43]

---

[42] Psalm 121.
[43] From traditional *Siddur* prayer book liturgy.

Prayer of the Repentant:

O God, I have erred, sinned and willfully transgressed before You, and I have done that which is evil in Your eyes, especially with the sin(s) of … (*state the specific sins or errors*).

I am sincerely ashamed of my sins, and I repent and firmly undertake not to do so again.

Please God, in Your infinite grace and compassion forgive my sins and transgressions and grant me atonement, as it is written: "Let the wicked abandon his way and the man of iniquity his thoughts; and let him return unto God, and He will show him compassion, and to our God, for He will pardon abundantly."[44] And it is written: "Do I desire at all that the wicked should die, says the Lord, God; it is rather that he return from his ways and live!"[45]

---

[44] Isaiah 55:7.
[45] Ezekiel 18:23.

For the choirmaster, a Psalm by David, when Nathan the prophet came to him after he had gone to Bathsheba. Be gracious to me, O God, in keeping with Your kindness; in accordance with Your abounding compassion, erase my transgressions. Cleanse me thoroughly of my wrongdoing, and purify me of my sin. For I acknowledge my transgressions, and my sin is always before me. Against You alone have I sinned, and done that which is evil in Your eyes; [forgive me] so that You will be justified in Your verdict, vindicated in Your judgment. Indeed, I was begotten in iniquity, and in sin did my mother conceive me. Indeed, You desire truth in the innermost parts; teach me the wisdom of concealed things. Purge me with hyssop and I shall be pure; cleanse me and I shall be whiter than snow. Let me hear joy and gladness; then the bones that You have shattered will rejoice. Hide Your face from my sins, and erase all my trespasses. Create in me a pure heart, O God, and renew within me an upright spirit. Do not cast me out from before You, and do not take Your Spirit of Holiness away from me. Restore to me the joy of Your deliverance, and support me with a spirit of generosity. I will teach transgressors Your ways, and sinners will return to You. Save me from bloodguilt, O God,

God of my deliverance; my tongue will sing joyously of Your righteousness. My Lord, open my lips, and my mouth shall declare Your praise. For You do not desire that I bring sacrifices, nor do You wish burnt offerings. The offering [desirable] to God is a contrite spirit; a contrite and broken heart, God, You do not disdain. In Your goodwill, bestow goodness upon Zion; rebuild the walls of Jerusalem. Then You will desire offerings of righteousness, burnt-offering and whole-offering; then they will offer bulls upon Your altar.[46]

Verses of placing trust in God, before sleeping:

When you lie down, you will not be afraid; you will lie down and your sleep will be sweet.[47]

May I sleep well; may I awake in mercy.[48]

I entrust my spirit into Your hand; You will redeem me God, God of truth![49]

---

[46] Psalm 51.
[47] Proverbs 3:24.
[48] From traditional *Siddur* prayer book liturgy.
[49] Psalms 31:6.

Blessings Before Eating or Drinking[50]

Before a person eats or drinks, it is proper to say words of praise and blessing to God, as thanks for that which God has provided for his needs and enjoyment.

Recommended versions of the traditional blessings before eating or drinking are given here. These six blessings correspond to the various categories of food. (Upon hearing these specific blessings said to God by others, it is correct to respond "Amen.")

i. Before eating bread:

Blessed are You, Lord our God, King of the universe, Who brings forth bread from the earth.

Examples: bread, bagels, pita bread, and rolls – if the flour is from wheat, barley, rye, oats or spelt, mixed with water as the main liquid.

---

[50] For Rules of Blessings before partaking of foods or beverages, see p. 47.

ii. Before eating other cooked foods made from grain flour, or rice:

Blessed are You, Lord our God, King of the universe, Who creates various kinds of sustenance.

Examples: cakes, cereals, cookies, crackers, pastries, pasta, cream of wheat, cooked rice, rice cakes.

iii. Before drinking grape wine or grape juice:

Blessed are You, Lord our God, King of the universe, Who creates the fruit of the vine.

iv. Before eating fruit of a tree:

Blessed are You, Lord our God, King of the universe, Who creates the fruit of the tree.

Examples: fruit of *perennial* trees, bushes, cacti and woody vines, such as apples, blueberries, cranberries, grapes, and nuts (except peanuts).

v. Before eating produce of other plants:

Blessed are You, Lord our God, King of the universe, Who creates the fruit of the earth.

Examples: edible roots (e.g. peanuts), leafy greens, all vegetables, and annual or perennial herbaceous fruit (e.g. bananas, artichokes, melons, strawberries, pineapples).

vi. Before any other type of food or beverage:

Blessed are You, Lord our God, King of the universe, by Whose word all things came to be.

Examples: cheeses, eggs, meats, mushrooms, fully processed foods (e.g. peanut butter, tofu, candy), beverages (except grape wine or grape juice), and any type of food not included in the examples above.

(Use this blessing if in doubt as to which one of the above blessings applies.)

Other Blessings of Thanks to God

These are other pleasures for which blessings of thanks to God were composed by the Sages.

When smelling sweet spices (e.g., cinnamon):

Blessed are You, Lord our God, King of the universe, Who creates various kinds of spices.

On hearing news that is good for both oneself and others:

Blessed are You, Lord our God, King of the universe, Who is good and does good.

After a miracle occurs for a person, if he returns to that place after an interval of a month or more, he may recite:

Blessed are You, Lord our God, King of the universe, Who performed a miracle for me in this place.

If miracles were also done for him in other places, he may include those as well, by saying:

Blessed are You, Lord our God, King of the universe, Who performed a miracle for me in this place, and in [such-and-such a place; and in such-and-such a place …].

Rules of Blessings for Foods or Beverages

1. A blessing may be said even if only a small amount of food or beverage will be consumed.

2. Before beginning to recite one of the listed blessings (i) – (vi) for a food, one should know which one is the correct blessing to say.

3. After beginning to recite a blessing, do not interrupt with other words until the first bite or drink is swallowed.

4. Since names of God are part of the blessings, and it is forbidden to say God's names in vain, one should only say them under the necessary conditions. (When teaching them to a child, one may pronounce God's names if needed, until the child has learned the words.)

5. One should answer "Amen" immediately after hearing a blessing made by another person, if he is sure that the person is blessing only the One God. (But one does

not conclude with "Amen" after his own blessing.)

6. If several different foods in the same category will be eaten, say only one blessing that will cover all of them. For example, when eating apples and oranges, say the blessing (iv) only once, and intend to include all the fruit.

7. When blessing (vi) is said for a food, non-grape beverages that will be drunk are included as well.

8. If different categories of foods will be eaten without bread, the order of reciting blessings for each type of food is in the order of the blessings listed above. For example, when beginning to eat a mixed salad, first say the blessing for avocado [blessing (iv), thus including all fruits], then for tomato [blessing (v), thus including all vegetables], and then for cheese [blessing (vi), thus including all other types of food].

9. For a dish that contains a primary food mixed together with secondary foods of different types, only the blessing for the primary food is said. For example, say only blessing (i) for raisin bread, and only blessing (ii) for apple pie.

10. If the correct specific blessing is unknown, in doubt or forgotten, blessing (vi) can be said for any dish, to cover everything.

11. *When starting a meal with the blessing for bread,* the blessing (i) can cover the entire meal (since all foods are secondary to bread), so blessings are not said for the other foods or drinks. (But grape wine or grape juice always receives its own blessing, even during a meal with bread.)

12. After saying the blessing over grape wine or grape juice, an additional blessing for any other beverages is not necessary, since all other beverages are secondary (just as the blessing over bread exempts other foods and non-grape beverages).

Grace after a Meal

After a person eats or drinks a satisfying amount, it is fitting to thank and bless God for giving him his sustenance.

It is customary to recite a prayer of "Grace" after eating a filling meal, but not after eating only a small amount of food.

When saying Grace after a meal, it is proper to include thanks to God for other necessities – for example, health, livelihood and existence.

The two paragraphs starting on the next page, arranged by the author for Gentiles, are recommended.

There are also shorter options for Grace after a meal, such as:

the original short form
(*as taught by Abraham to his guests*):

Blessed is the God of the universe, from Whose bounty we have eaten.

an alternative short form
(*especially for young children*):

Blessed is the Lord our God, King of the universe, Master of this bread.

Recommended prayer for Grace after a Meal

We offer thanks to You, Master of the universe, Who in His great goodness, provides sustenance for the entire world with grace, with kindness, and with mercy. He gives food to all flesh, for His kindness is everlasting.[51] Through His great goodness to us continuously, we do not lack food,[52] and may we never lack food, for the sake of His great Name. For He, benevolent God, provides nourishment and sustenance for all, does good to all, and prepares food for all His creatures whom He has created, as it is said: You open Your hand and satisfy the desire of every living thing.[53] Blessed is the God of the universe, from Whose bounty we have eaten.

Please, Master of the universe, in Your mercy give us life and health, livelihood, and sustenance, so that we may thank and

---

[51] Psalms 136:25.
[52] Having just completed a meal.
[53] Psalms 145:16.

bless You always. Please do not make us dependent upon the gifts of mortal men nor upon their loans, but only upon Your full, open, and generous hand, that we may never be shamed or disgraced. Give thanks to the Lord for He is good, for His kindness is everlasting.[54] Blessed is the man who trusts in the Lord, and the Lord will be his security.[55]

One may add further requests to God as desired.

---

[54] Ibid. 136:1.
[55] Jeremiah 17:7.

7 Verses for Noahide Children to Learn

Rabbi J. Immanuel Schochet recommended these seven verses for Noahide children to learn and recite. We urge all Noahide children to memorize them, and say them every night before bedtime. (They are easier to learn when sung with tunes.)

1) Genesis 1:1. In the beginning God created the heavens and the earth.

2) Genesis 5:1. On the day that God created Adam, He made him in the image of God.

3) Psalms 34:15. Turn away from bad and do good; seek peace and pursue it.

4) Psalms 145:9. The Lord is good to all, and His mercies extend over all His works.

5) Proverbs 15:3. The eyes of the Lord are everywhere, seeing the bad and the good.

6) Job 28:28. Behold, the fear of the Lord is wisdom, and turning away from bad is understanding.

7) Isaiah 48:17. Thus said the Lord, your Redeemer, the Holy One of Israel: I am the Lord, your God, Who teaches you for your benefit, Who guides you in the way you should go.

Parents and teachers may add other verses from the Hebrew Bible as they feel are appropriate.

Part III

Prayers for Specific Needs and Requests

A Prayer for Livelihood:[56]

May it be Your Will, Lord, our God, that my provisions and my livelihood, and the provisions and livelihood of my household, be encompassing, appropriate and virtuous in Your hands. May we never be in need of the gifts of man nor of their loans, but only of Your hand which is full, open, holy and generous. And may my work and all my dealings be blessed and not destitute, for life and not for death. And may I merit that no desecration of the Name of Heaven occur through me, and that I may be among the charitable and those that influence for good to everyone at all times, and fill my hand with Your blessings and satiate me of Your goodness. For You are blessed and bring blessings to the universe. The eyes of all look expectantly to You, and You give them

---

[56] Adapted from the prayer by Rabbi Moses Cordovero.

all their food in its proper time. You open Your hand, and satisfy the desire of every living being.[57] Cast your burden upon the Lord, and He will sustain you; He will never allow the faltering of the righteous.[58] Please lift my strength and raise my fortune in order that I will be able to serve You wholeheartedly all the days of the world. Amen.

---

[57] Psalms 145:16.
[58] Psalms 55:23.

Prayer for Travelers[59]

This is said outside the city one is leaving, on the first day of the trip. On subsequent days of the trip until returning home, it may be recited every morning; on those days, some conclude instead with "Blessed are You, Who hears prayer."

May it be Your will, Lord our God, to lead us in peace and direct our steps in peace, to guide us in peace, to support us in peace, and to bring us to our destination in life, joy, and peace
(*if one intends to return on the same day, add*:
and return us in peace).
Deliver us from the hands of every enemy and lurking foe, from robbers and wild beasts on the journey, and from all kinds of calamities that may come and afflict the world; and bestow blessing upon all our actions. Grant me grace, kindness, and mercy in Your eyes and in the eyes of all who behold us, and bestow bountiful kindness upon us. Hear the voice of our prayer, for You hear everyone's prayer. Blessed are You, God, Who hears prayer.

---

[59] From *Siddur Tehillat HaShem with English Translation, Annotated Ed.*, p. 85, pub. Kehot.

Prayer for a Sick Person

In addition to Psalm 20 (p. 26), and any other Psalms recited in prayer for the sick person, one may say the following prayer.

For a male: May the Holy One, blessed be He, be filled with mercy for (*mention the sick person's given names*), son of (*use* Noah *if the sick person is a Gentile; use* Sarah *if the sick person is a Jew*), to restore him to health and to cure him, to strengthen him and to invigorate him. And may God hasten to send him from Heaven a complete recovery to all his bodily parts and veins, a healing of spirit and a healing of body. Amen.

For a female: May the Holy One, blessed be He, be filled with mercy for (*mention the sick person's given names*), daughter of (*for a Gentile, use* Noah; *for a Jew, use* Sarah), to restore her to health and to cure her, to strengthen her and to invigorate her. And may God hasten to send her from Heaven a complete recovery to all her bodily parts and veins, a healing of spirit and a healing of body. Amen.

It is appropriate to donate to a proper charity, and to do other acts of goodness and kindness, for the sake of the healing of the sick person.

Prayer for a Newborn Gentile Baby

May God bless the woman who has given birth (*say her name, as above*), together with the child born to her (*say the child's given names*), son/daughter of (*say the father's name, as above*). May they bring him/her up to the Seven Commandments, marriage and good deeds.

Prayer for a Departed Soul

May God remember the soul of (*mention the deceased person's given names*), son/daughter of (*use Noah if the deceased is a Gentile; use Abraham if the deceased is a Jew*), who has gone on to his/her world. By virtue of my praying on his/her behalf, and, without making a vow, my intent to donate proper charity on his/her behalf, may his/her soul be bound in the Bond of Life together with the souls of the righteous, and let us say: Amen.

All or part of the above prayer may be recited (not more than once in the day) during a funeral, along with the following Psalm 23. It may also be recited at a memorial gathering, during the week of mourning, on an anniversary of a passing, or other special occasions that are deemed appropriate. All or part of Psalms 49 and/or 139 may also be recited.

A Psalm by David. The Lord is my shepherd, I shall not lack. He lays me down in green meadows; He leads me beside tranquil waters. He restores my soul. He directs me in paths of justice for the sake of His Name. Even if I will walk in the valley overshadowed by death, I will fear no evil, for You are with me. Your rod and your staff – they will comfort me. You will prepare a table for me in view of my tormentors. You have anointed my head with oil; my cup overflows. May only goodness and kindness pursue me all the days of my life, and I shall dwell in the House of the Lord for many long years.[60]

This booklet of prayers is dedicated to the growing number of Noahides and Noahide communities around the world.

---

[60] Psalm 23.

Printed in Great Britain
by Amazon